Multistep Math Problems with Written Explanations
Grade 6

Table of Contents

D1444306

Multistep Math Problems with Written Explanations
Grade 6

Introduction

This book is intended to give students the opportunity to practice solving multistep computations and word problems and to explain in writing the steps that they took in the process. These skills will prepare students for standardized tests and help them to achieve the standards set forth by the NCTM (National Council of Teachers of Mathematics). These exercises assume some prior experience or familiarity with the skills involved and are designed as enrichment tools for existing curriculum.

Written explanations compel students to reconsider their work and to understand the steps they took to find their answers. In the writing, they clarify to themselves and illustrate to others that they grasp the concepts in the exercises. Due to the subjective nature of written explanations, these may vary, but the end results should be the same for all students. Students will benefit from sharing their mathematical thinking with a partner, a small group, or the entire class.

Organization
Each lesson begins with guided practice and then provides problems for skill reinforcement. The lessons can be used as classwork or homework; however, working through the practice exercises as a group will allow students to ask questions. This will help students to grasp the concepts and gain confidence before they begin working individually or in pairs.

Unit 1: Number and Operations
In this unit, students write number sentences, select appropriate operations, organize steps in a process, and choose strategies to solve problems.

Unit 2: Algebra
In this unit, students make a table, translate variable equations, choose a method, and write number sentences using variables to represent unknown quantities.

Unit 3: Geometry
Students solve multistep problems dealing with areas of squares, rectangles, triangles, and circles, and find surface areas and volumes of boxes and cylinders using formulas.

Unit 4: Measurement
In this unit, students solve problems concerning capacity, weight, length, currency, and time. Problems ask students to choose a variable or work problems that require many steps.

Unit 5: Data Analysis and Probability
Students study line graphs, circle graphs, and Venn diagrams, as well as explore combinations and probability.

Assessments
There are two kinds of assessments.
- There is a general assessment that covers important material appropriate for the sixth grade on pages 3 and 4. It can be given as a pretest to gauge students' knowledge of the material to be covered in this book. Later in the year, the same test can be administered to determine students' understanding, progress, and achievement.
- Each unit also has an assessment. These unit assessments can be administered at any time during the unit as a pretest, review, or posttest for specific concepts.

Special Note
Students may need to use their own paper to work some of the problems and explain the steps they took to arrive at their answers.

Correlation to NCTM Standards
The NCTM has set specific standards to help students become confident in their mathematical abilities. Multistep problems and written explanations are important components of the mathematics curriculum because they represent an important extension of students' knowledge and understanding of mathematics. A thorough understanding of patterns, equations, representations, and variables heightens students' awareness of the usefulness of mathematics in everyday life. This book is designed to help parents and teachers guide students toward achievement of the standards for their grade level through problem solving, reasoning and proof, communication, connections, and representation. According to NCTM standards, students should be able to:
- build new mathematical knowledge through problem solving;
- solve problems that arise in mathematics and in other contexts;
- apply and adapt a variety of appropriate strategies to solve problems;
- organize and consolidate their mathematical thinking through communication;
- communicate their mathematical thinking coherently and clearly to peers, teachers, and others;
- analyze and evaluate the mathematical thinking and strategies of others;
- use the language of mathematics to express mathematical ideas precisely.

Overall Assessment

Directions Solve each problem. Explain the steps you took. ✎

1. Haley entered the elevator on the third floor. She traveled up 8 floors, down 4 floors, and down 2 more floors. On what floor did Haley leave the elevator?

   _____

   _____

   _____

2. On his first 4 tests, Eric earned 77, 83, 88, and 85. What must he earn on his fifth test to have an 85 average for all 5 tests?

   _____

   _____

   _____

3. Create an input-output table for the expression $3w$ using the values 4, 6, and 8 for w.

   _____

   _____

   _____

   _____

4. A pair of boots usually sells for $80.00. This week they are on sale for 25% off. Find the sale price.

   _____

   _____

   _____

5. A rectangular box is 5 inches by 7 inches by 10 inches. What is the total surface area of the box?

   _____

   _____

   _____

Go on to the next page.

Overall Assessment, page 2

Directions Solve each problem. Explain the steps you took. ✏️

6. A water barrel has a radius of 15 inches and a height of 35 inches. What is the volume of the barrel?

_____

_____

_____

7.   3 hr 16 min
      − 1 hr 48 min

8. Kurt has two kite strings. The red string is 50 m long. The green string is 0.075 km long. Which one is longer? By how much?

_____

_____

_____

9. Brandy has 7 hats. Three are green, 2 are red, and 2 are blue. If she chooses a hat at random, what is the probability she will choose a green hat?

_____

_____

_____

10. For lunch Daniel can choose fom 2 types of bread, 3 types of cheese, and 5 types of meat to make a sandwich. How many different combinations of 1 bread, 1 cheese, and 1 meat can Daniel make?

_____

_____

_____

Name _____ Date _____

Unit 1 Assessment: Number and Operations

Directions Solve each problem. Explain the steps you took. ✏️

1. Betsy entered the elevator on the fourth floor. She traveled up 5 floors, down 2 floors, and down 1 more before leaving the elevator. On what floor did Betsy leave the elevator?

   _____

   _____

   _____

2. $5 + 2 \times 3$

   _____

   _____

3. In his first 4 rounds of golf, Bill scored 85, 77, 82, and 80. What score must Bill achieve in his fifth round to have an average of 80 for all 5 rounds?

   _____

   _____

   _____

4. A train travels 225 miles in 3 hours. At this rate, how far can it go in 7 hours?

   _____

   _____

   _____

5. Jack has $3\frac{3}{4}$ cups of ice cream. If each serving is $\frac{3}{4}$ cup, how many servings can he make?

   _____

   _____

   _____

Name _____   Date _____

Integers

Integers are a set of numbers that consists of positive and negative whole numbers and zero. You can use integers to solve problems.

Here's How!

Step 1: Read the question.
Sue entered the elevator on the seventh floor. She traveled up 3 floors and then down 5 floors before leaving the elevator. On what floor did Sue exit the elevator?

Step 2: Write a number sentence. Start with the floor on which Sue entered the elevator.
$7 + 3 - 5 = n$

Step 3: Solve.
$7 + 3 - 5 = n$
$10 - 5 = n$
$5 = n$
Sue exited the elevator on the fifth floor.

Directions Solve each problem. Explain the steps you took. ✎

1. Josh entered the elevator at the lobby. He went up 6 floors and then down 2 before leaving the elevator. On what floor did Josh end up? (Hint: The lobby is on the first floor.)

   Number sentence _____

   Solution _____

   Explanation _____

2. Rich got on the elevator on the twelfth floor. He rode down 2 floors and then up 4 floors before leaving the elevator. On what floor did Rich leave the elevator?

   Number sentence _____

   Solution _____

   Explanation _____

3. Jim entered the elevator from the third floor. He rode up 8 floors, down 2 floors, and then up another 3 floors before exiting. On what floor did Jim exit the elevator?

   Number sentence _____

   Solution _____

   Explanation _____

Go on to the next page.

Integers, page 2

Directions Solve each problem. Explain the steps you took.

4. James entered the elevator on the ninth floor. He rode up 5 floors, down 6 floors, and then down another 2 floors before leaving the elevator. On what floor did James leave the elevator?

   Number sentence _____

   Solution _____

   Explanation _____

5. Christina got on the elevator at the lobby. She rode up 14 floors, down 6 floors, up 4 floors, and then she exited the elevator. On what floor did Christina exit the elevator?

   Number sentence _____

   Solution _____

   Explanation _____

6. Evan entered the elevator on the fifth floor. He rode down 1 floor, down 3 more floors, and up 4 floors before leaving. On what floor did Evan leave the elevator?

   Number sentence _____

   Solution _____

   Explanation _____

7. Carly got on the elevator on the first floor. She rode up 6 floors, down 3 floors, and then up 2 floors before exiting. On what floor did Carly exit the elevator?

   Number sentence _____

   Solution _____

   Explanation _____

8. Erica got on the elevator at the fifth floor. She went up 3 floors and then down 2 floors before leaving the elevator. On what floor did Erica leave the elevator?

   Number sentence _____

   Solution _____

   Explanation _____

Name _____ Date _____

Order of Operations

The order of operations is a set of rules used to solve problems with more
than one operation. The order of operations is given below.
First, do operations inside parentheses.
Second, multiply and divide from left to right.
Third, add and subtract from left to right.
You can remember the order of operations by using the acronym
Please **M**y **D**ear **A**unt **S**ally (**P**arentheses, **M**ultiplication, **D**ivision, **A**ddition, **S**ubtraction).

Here's How!

Example 1: $4 \times (5 - 3)$

Step 1: Do operations inside parentheses.
$4 \times (5 - 3)$
4×2

Step 2: Multiply from left to right.
4×2
8

Example 2: $8 + 6 \div 2$

Step 1: Divide from left to right.
$8 + 6 \div 2$
$8 + 3$

Step 2: Add from left to right.
11

Directions Solve each problem. Explain the steps you took.

1. $(4 + 6) \div 2$

_____

_____

2. $8 + 3 \times 5$

_____

_____

3. $3 + 8 - 9$

_____

_____

4. $5 \times (10 - 6)$

_____

_____

5. $6 - 3 \times 2$

_____

_____

6. $4 \div (1 + 1)$

_____

_____

Go on to the next page.

Order of Operations, page 2

The order of operations is a set of rules used to solve problems with
more than one operation. The order of operations is given below.
First, do operations inside parentheses.
Second, multiply and divide from left to right.
Third, add and subtract from left to right.

Directions Solve each problem. Explain the steps you took. ✏️

7. $8 - 6 + 4$

_____

_____

8. $19 - 2 \times 3$

_____

_____

9. $15 \div (4 + 1)$

_____

_____

10. $(8 + 2) \div 2$

_____

_____

11. $4 \times (18 - 9)$

_____

_____

12. $6 \div 2 \times 8$

_____

_____

13. Rewrite Exercise 2 so that the answer is 55.

_____

_____

Averages

An average is found by adding all of the amounts and dividing the total by the number of amounts. Sometimes it is necessary to find a number to help a set of numbers reach a certain average.

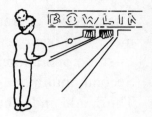

Here's How!

Step 1:   Read the problem.
The following numbers of students went to the first 5 basketball games: 180, 200, 175, 200, 205. How many students must attend the sixth game in order to have an average of 200 students per game?

Step 2:   Add the numbers of students at the first 5 games.
180 + 200 + 175 + 200 + 205 = 960

Step 3:   Multiply the average by the total number of games.
200 × 6 = 1,200

Step 4:   Subtract the answer in step 2 from the answer in step 3.
1,200 − 960 = 240
240 students must attend the sixth game.

Directions Solve each problem. Explain the steps you took. ✐

1. Sara received scores of 79, 83, 76, and 100 on her first 4 math tests. What score must she get on her fifth test to have an average of 85 for all 5 tests?

   _____

   _____

   _____

2. Kevin bowled scores of 112, 126, 98, and 118 in his first 4 games. What score must he bowl in his fifth game to have an average of 120 for all 5 games?

   _____

   _____

   _____

Go on to the next page.

Averages, page 2

3. In his first 5 rounds of golf, James scored 84, 71, 77, 68, and 74. What score must James achieve in his sixth round in order to have an average of 75 for all 6 rounds?

_____

_____

_____

4. Matthew scored 89, 93, 100, 77, and 81 on his first 5 science tests. What score must he earn on his sixth test in order to have an average of 90 for all 6 tests?

_____

_____

_____

5. In her first 5 games, Elizabeth bowled 128, 116, 104, 112, and 134. What must she bowl in her sixth game in order to have an average of 120 for all 6 games?

_____

_____

_____

6. The following numbers of moviegoers saw the first 6 showings of a recently released movie: 213, 322, 278, 309, 258, 296. How many movie fans must attend the seventh showing in order to have an average of 280 people per showing?

_____

_____

_____

7. The following numbers of students ride the first 5 buses to leave Peachtree Middle School: 73, 71, 68, 62, 74. If the average number of students on each bus is 70, how many students ride the sixth bus?

_____

_____

_____

8. Hunter's first 5 math grades are 94, 88, 92, 96, and 80. What does he need to make for the sixth math grade to have a 90 average for the year?

_____

_____

_____

Solving Problems in Parts

Some difficult problems can be made easier if they are broken into smaller parts.

Here's How!

Step 1: Read the problem.
Rebecca jogs 3 miles each day. Her brother, Alex, skates twice as far as Rebecca jogs each day. After 7 days, how many more miles does Alex skate?

Step 2: Find out how far Rebecca jogs in 7 days.
$3 \times 7 = 21$

Step 3: Find out how far Alex skates in 7 days.
$3 \times 2 \times 7 = 42$

Step 4: Subtract to find how many more miles Alex skates.
$42 - 21 = 21$
Alex skates 21 more miles than Rebecca jogs in 7 days.

Directions Solve each problem. Explain the steps you took. ✏️

1. A sight-seeing boat makes 4 trips each day. It travels 9 miles on each trip. How many miles does it travel in 6 days?

   _____

   _____

   _____

2. Richard drove 132 miles. His father drove twice as many miles. How many miles did they travel altogether?

   _____

   _____

   _____

Go on to the next page.

Solving Problem in Parts, page 2

Directions Solve each problem. Explain the steps you took. ✏️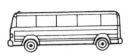

3. Tina's family bought 12 rolls of film for their vacation. There are 24 pictures on each roll of film. If they used all except 3 rolls, how many pictures did they take?

    _____

    _____

    _____

4. On her hiking trip, Kay hiked 7 hours each day. She hiked 4 miles each hour. How many days did it take Kay to hike 168 miles?

    _____

    _____

    _____

5. A bus tour will cover 450 miles each day for 5 days. If each driver can drive only 250 miles, how many drivers will be needed?

    _____

    _____

    _____

6. A train travels 186 miles in 3 hours. At this rate, how many hours will it take the train to go 868 miles?

    _____

    _____

    _____

7. Jack rode his bike 18 miles each day. Sam rode his bike half as far as Jack did each day. After 5 days, how many more miles had Jack ridden?

    _____

    _____

    _____

8. A plane travels 1,575 miles in 3 hours. At this rate, how many miles will it travel in 7 hours?

    _____

    _____

    _____

Name _____   Date _____

Fraction Problem Solving

To solve problems with more than one step that include fractions, work one step at a time. Check the computation in each step before going on.

Here's How!

Step 1: Read the problem.
The Garden Club has decided to make a terrarium. Ferns will take up $\frac{1}{3}$ and grass will take up $\frac{1}{8}$ of the total area. Flowers will take up the rest. What fractional part of the terrarium will be flowers?

Step 2: Find common denominators, and add the fractions for ferns and grass.
$\frac{1}{3} + \frac{1}{8} = \frac{8}{24} + \frac{3}{24} = \frac{11}{24}$

Step 3: Subtract $\frac{11}{24}$ from 1 to find the fraction for flowers.
$1 - \frac{11}{24} = \frac{24}{24} - \frac{11}{24} = \frac{13}{24}$

So, $\frac{13}{24}$ of the terrarium will be flowers.

Directions Solve each problem. Explain the steps you took. ✏️

1. Alex had $3\frac{1}{3}$ cups of popcorn. It takes $\frac{2}{3}$ cup to make 1 serving. How many servings can he make?

_____

_____

_____

2. Dave worked $3\frac{1}{3}$ hours on Friday and $2\frac{3}{4}$ hours on Saturday. Colleen worked $1\frac{5}{8}$ hours on Friday and $4\frac{1}{2}$ hours on Saturday. How much less time did Dave work than Colleen?

_____

_____

_____

Go on to the next page.

Fraction Problem Solving, page 2

Directions Solve each problem. Explain the steps you took. ✐

3. There are $9\frac{1}{3}$ cups of milk left in the carton. How many servings of $1\frac{1}{3}$ cup are there?

_____

_____

4. Kelsey had some wire that was $5\frac{3}{8}$ feet long. She used $1\frac{1}{2}$ feet for one project and $2\frac{1}{4}$ feet for another project. How much of the wire was left?

_____

_____

5. A recital is $2\frac{1}{6}$ hours long. The first piece is $1\frac{1}{2}$ hours long, and intermission is $\frac{1}{5}$ hour long. How long is the rest of the recital?

_____

_____

6. Ellen spent $\frac{2}{7}$ of her earnings on clothes and $\frac{3}{14}$ of her earnings on shoes. She saved the rest. What fractional part of her earnings did she save?

_____

_____

7. Trucker's Heaven Diner uses hundreds of plates, glasses, and cups each day. The dishwashers start a new load of dishes every $1\frac{1}{4}$ hours. If the dishwashers work for $7\frac{1}{2}$ hours, how many loads of dishes do they wash in that time?

_____

_____

8. In a race, $\frac{1}{3}$ of the swimmers finished in less than 15 minutes. $\frac{5}{9}$ of the swimmers finished within 20 to 30 minutes. The rest of the swimmers did not finish. What fractional part of the swimmers did not finish?

_____

_____

Name _____ Date _____

Unit 2 Assessment: Algebra

Directions Solve each problem. Explain the steps you took. ✏️

1. Create an input-output table for the expression $w - 5$ using the values 12, 14, and 16.

   _____

   _____

   _____

2. Translate the sentence below into an algebraic equation. Then, solve.
   Five more than a number n is 7.

   _____

   _____

3. Find the unit prices of the items. Then, tell which is a better buy.
   A 6-pack of juice boxes for $1.98 or a 12-pack of juice boxes for $3.72

   _____

   _____

   _____

4. Keith bought 4 shirts for $24.00. How much would 3 shirts cost?

   _____

   _____

5. A coat usually sells for $75.00. This week it is 20% off. Find the sale price.

   _____

   _____

   _____

6. A video game costs $27.50. If the sales tax rate is 7%, what is the total cost of the video game?

   _____

   _____

   _____

Input-Output Tables

With an *input-output* table, you can evaluate an algebraic expression using as many values as you want.

Here's How!

Step 1: Make an input-output table.

Step 2: Substitute the input values for the variables.

Step 3: Simplify the algebraic expressions

Input	Expression	Output
w	$w + 14$	
2	$2 + 14$	16
5	$5 + 14$	19
8	$8 + 14$	22

Directions Complete the input-output tables. Explain the steps as you go. ✏️

1.

Input	Expression	Output
w	$w + 3$	
7		
8		
9		

2.

Input	Expression	Output
w	$w - 8$	
13		
15		
19		

3.

Input	Expression	Output
w	$4w$	
7		
8		
9		

4.

Input	Expression	Output
w	$w \div 6$	
18		
24		
36		

Go on to the next page.

Input-Output Tables, page 2

Directions Make an input-output table for each algebraic expression. Evaluate each expression for 8, 12, 16. Explain the steps you took. ✐

5. $w + 25$

6. $w - 7$

7. $3w$

8. $\frac{w}{4}$

9. $2w + 1$

10. $3w - 2$

Name _____ Date _____

Algebraic Equations

It may be helpful to translate a sentence into an equation before trying to solve. Sentences can be translated into equations just as word expressions can be translated into algebraic expressions.

Sentence	Equation
Three more than a number, n, is 16.	$n + 3 = 16$
Eight less than a number, t, is 7.	$t - 8 = 7$
Four times a number, t, is 16.	$4t = 16$
The quotient of a number, y, and 5 is 4.	$\frac{y}{5} = 4$

Here's How!

Step 1: Read the sentence.
Five more than a number, x, is 8.

Step 2: Translate to a variable equation.
$x + 5 = 8$

Step 3: Solve.

$$\begin{array}{rcr} x + 5 &=& 8 \\ -5 &=& -5 \\ \hline x &=& 3 \end{array}$$

Directions Write an equation for each sentence. Then, solve the equation. Explain the steps you took.

1. Three less than a number, r, is 8.

   Equation _____

   Solution _____

2. A number, k, multiplied by 5 is 25.

   Equation _____

   Solution _____

3. The sum of five and a number, u, is 14.

   Equation _____

   Solution _____

4. A number, w, divided by 3 is 7.

   Equation _____

   Solution _____

Algebraic Equations, page 2

Directions → Write an equation for each sentence. Then, solve the equation. Explain the steps you took. ✎

5. The quotient of a number, *d*, and 6 is 48.

Equation _____

Solution _____

6. Thirty-three less than a number, *w*, is forty.

Equation _____

Solution _____

7. A number, *f*, divided by 7 is 12.

Equation _____

Solution _____

8. Fourteen plus a number, *c*, is 18.3.

Equation _____

Solution _____

9. Twice a number, *k*, is 36.

Equation _____

Solution _____

10. A number, *r*, plus 6.3 is 12.5.

Equation _____

Solution _____

11. Twice a number, *h*, is 56.

Equation _____

Solution _____

12. A number, *m*, plus 7 is 18.

Equation _____

Solution _____

Choosing the Operation

Writing a number sentence can be helpful in solving word problems. Choosing the operation before working the problem will help simplify the problem.

Here's How!

Step 1: Read the problem.
Mary packs 10 flashlights in each supply pack.
How many flashlights are there in 4 supply packs?

Step 2: Choose the operation.
Multiplication

Step 3: Write a number sentence.
$10 \times 4 = n$

Step 4: Solve.
$10 \times 4 = 40$
There are 40 flashlights in 4 supply packs.

Directions Follow the steps above to solve each problem. Explain the steps you took. ✏️

1. Karen's family took 37 photographs during the first week of their camping trip. They took 45 photographs during the second week. How many photographs did they take in all?

   Operation _____

   Number sentence _____

   Solution _____

2. A group of mountain climbers have to climb 48 meters to reach a cliff. If they can climb 1 meter in 2 minutes, how many minutes will it take them to reach the cliff?

   Operation _____

   Number sentence _____

   Solution _____

3. Mindy's scout troop went hiking. They packed 36 backpacks with 2 sandwiches in each. How many sandwiches did they have?

   Operation _____

   Number sentence _____

   Solution _____

Go on to the next page.

Name _____   Date _____

Choosing the Operation, page 2

Directions → Solve each problem. Explain the steps you took. ✏

4. In the evening, 40 people went to look at the stars through telescopes. There were 8 telescopes. How many people shared each telescope?

   Operation _____

   Number sentence _____

   Solution _____

5. Sixty hikers climbed up to the Aztec ruins. There are 5 paths to the ruins. If the same number of hikers took each path, how many people took each path?

   Operation _____

   Number sentence _____

   Solution _____

6. There are 28 cabins at the campsite. If each cabin holds 5 people, how many people in all can the campsite house?

   Operation _____

   Number sentence _____

   Solution _____

7. Mary and Amy collected 25 fossils on their hike. If Amy collected 8, how many did Mary collect?

   Operation _____

   Number sentence _____

   Solution _____

8. The campers brought 4 canoes on their trip. If each canoe can carry 3 people, how many people can go canoeing at one time?

   Operation _____

   Number sentence _____

   Solution _____

Name _____   Date _____

Unit Price

Many products are sold in packages of more than 1 item. Unit price is the cost per item. To find unit price, divide the cost per package by the number of units in the package.

Here's How!

Step 1: Read the problem.
Find the cost of each watermelon slice if 3 slices cost $3.75.

Step 2: Divide the price by the number of units.
$3.75 ÷ 3 = $1.25
Each slice of watermelon costs $1.25.

Directions Find the unit price for each item. Explain the steps you took. ✏

1. 4 bars of soap for $1.24 _____

2. 3 ballpoint pens for $0.99 _____

3. 12 bottles of juice for $6.96 _____

4. 8 yogurt bars for $1.28 _____

Directions In problems 5 through 11, find the unit price of each item. Then, tell which is the better buy. ✏

5. A 5-pound box of laundry soap for $4.95 or a 10-pound box for $8.50

_____

6. A package of 12 hamburger buns for $1.44 or a package of 8 for $0.88

_____

7. A package of 4 light bulbs for $3.72 or a package of 6 for $5.34

_____

8. A 6-ounce can of tomatoes for $0.54 or a 16-ounce can for $1.60

_____

9. A box of 10 envelopes for $0.80 or a box of 12 for $1.08

_____

10. A set of 8 drinking glasses for $6.56 or a set of 10 for $7.90

_____

11. A 36-ounce bottle of grape juice for $1.08 or a 12-ounce bottle for $0.48

Organizing Data

Sometimes when you are solving complex problems, it is helpful to work the problem in parts. Organize the data to make the problem easier.

Hern's One-Week Sale! *Big Savings*			
Gloves:	$8.75	Ties:	$11.00
Hats:	$9.50	Wool Skirts:	$22.00
Scarves:	$7.50	Umbrellas:	$14.00
Stockings:	$3.99	Flannel Shirts:	$12.00
Corduroy Pants:	$17.00	Socks:	5 pairs for $10.00

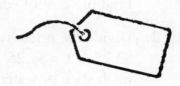

Directions Use the chart above to answer each question. Explain the steps you took. ✏️

1. How much will it cost Candy to buy a pair of gloves, a scarf, and 2 wool skirts?

   _____

   _____

2. Cindy plans to buy 10 pairs of socks, 2 scarves, and a flannel shirt. If she has $50.00, how much will she have left?

   _____

   _____

3. How much will it cost Maria to buy a tie for each of her 3 sons and a hat for her husband?

   _____

   _____

4. Jim returns a $33.99 jacket for credit. He buys 3 pairs of corduroy pants and uses the credit to pay for part of the purchase price. How much did he have to pay in addition to his store credit?

   _____

   _____

5. Kim wants to buy an umbrella for herself and 1 for her sister. Her mother also wants an umbrella and a pair of gloves. She gave Kim $25.00 for her purchases. How much more money does Kim need?

   _____

   _____

Finding Proportions

Proportions are used to solve problems with 2 equal ratios. Proportions are helpful in finding an unknown value. Use cross-products to find proportions.

Here's How!

Step 1: Read the problem.
Jake can buy 8 apples for $2. How much will 4 apples cost?

Step 2: Write a number sentence.
$\frac{8}{\$2} = \frac{4}{x}$

Step 3: Find the cross-products.
$8x = \$2 \times 4$
$8x = \$8$
$x = \$1$
Jake can buy 4 apples for $1.

Directions Solve each problem. Explain the steps you took.

1. Kevin can buy 5 oranges for $1. How much would 20 oranges cost?

_____

2. Mr. Barnes uses 1 quart of paint to make 4 signs for his store. How many quarts of paint would he need to make 10 signs?

_____

3. Sarah can jog 2 miles in 30 minutes. At this same rate, how long would it take her to jog 3 miles?

_____

4. Chris was paid $56 for 4 hours of work. How much would he receive for working 36 hours?

_____

5. It takes 618 bricks to build 100 square feet of wall. A crew of masons on the project laid 2,163 bricks on Monday. How many square feet of wall did they build?

_____

6. Ruth saves $2 of every $25 she earns. If she earns $1,750 per month, how much does she save?

_____

Percent Discount

When an item goes on sale, it is often discounted by a certain percentage. In order to find the sale price, you must find the discount and subtract it from the original price.

Here's How!

Step 1: Read the problem.
A camera sells for $161.25. With a discount of 30%, what is the sale price?

Step 2: Write an equation to help solve.
$161.25 – (30% of $161.25) = sale price

Step 3: Find the discount. Remember to change the percent to a decimal.
$0.30 \times $161.25 = $48.375
Round the discount to the nearest cent. $48.38

Step 4: Subtract the discount from the original price.
$161.25 – $48.38 = $112.87
The sale price is $112.87.

Directions Solve each problem. Round the discount to the nearest cent when necessary. Explain the steps you took. ✎

1. A video game usually sells for $32.69. This week it is 25% off. Find the sale price.

   Discount _____

   Sale price _____

2. A leather jacket usually sells for $107.25. It now sells for 20% off. Find the sale price.

   Discount _____

   Sale price _____

3. A pair of running shoes costs $49.50. After a 15% discount, how much do they cost?

   Discount _____

   Sale price _____

4. A DVD player costs $148.75. After a discount of 20%, how much does it cost?

   Discount _____

   Sale price _____

Name _____ Date _____

Percent Tax

Sales tax is added to most items you purchase. Sales tax is calculated based on a percentage of the price. In order to find the total price, you must find the amount of the tax and add it to the original price.

Here's How!

Step 1: Read the problem.
A videocassette tape sells for $10.95. A sales tax of 7% must be added to the cost. What is the total cost?

Step 2: Write an equation to help solve.
$10.95 + (7% of $10.95) = total cost

Step 3: Find the tax. Remember to change the percent to a decimal.
0.07 × $10.95 = $0.7665
Round the tax to the nearest cent. $0.77

Step 4: Add the tax to the original price.
$10.95 + $0.77 = $11.72
The total cost is $11.72.

Directions Solve each problem. Round the tax to the nearest cent when necessary. Explain the steps you took.

1. A box set of CDs is $21.25. The sales tax rate is 5%. What is the total cost of the box set?

    Tax _____

    Total Cost _____

2. The price of a video game is $43.75. A sales tax of 6% must be added. What is the total cost of the video game?

    Tax _____

    Total Cost _____

3. A pair of jeans costs $38.50. The sales tax rate is 4%. What is the total cost of the jeans?

    Tax _____

    Total Cost _____

4. The price of a pair of boots is $69.25. If the sales tax rate is 8%, what is the total cost of the boots?

    Tax _____

    Total Cost _____

Name _____   Date _____

Unit 3 Assessment: Geometry

1. Samantha is framing a painting. The width is 36 inches and the height is 48 inches. How many inches of framing will she need?

   _____

   _____

   _____

2. A lawn sprinkler has a radius of 6 feet. How many square feet can the sprinkler cover?

   _____

   _____

   _____

3. A rectangular box is 8 inches by 4 inches by 10 inches. What is the total surface area of the box?

   _____

   _____

   _____

4. A cube has a height of 5 inches. What is the volume of the cube?

   _____

   _____

   _____

5. A paint can has a radius of 4 inches and a height of 10 inches. What is the volume of the can?

   _____

   _____

   _____

Perimeter and Area Formulas

A formula is an equation that can be used for many problems that are alike. Replace the variables in the formula with the values you are given. Then, solve the equation for the missing value.

Helpful formulas:

Perimeter	Area
P = sum of lengths of sides (any polygon)	$A = lw$ (rectangle)
$P = 2l + 2w$ (rectangle)	$A = s^2$ (square)
$P = 4s$ (square)	$A = \frac{1}{2} bh$ (triangle)

Here's How!

Step 1: Read the question.
Kathleen is making a quilt. The final dimensions of the quilt will be 6 feet by 4 feet. What will the area of the quilt be?

Step 2: Determine the shape of the quilt.
Rectangle

Step 3: Choose the correct formula.
$A = lw$

Step 4: Replace l with 6 and w with 4. Solve.
$A = lw$
$A = 6 \times 4$
$A = 24$ square feet

Directions Solve each problem. Explain the steps you took. ✐

1. Mr. Leach wants to cover his bulletin board with blue paper. The board measures 5 ft on each side. How many square feet of paper will Mr. Leach need?

   Shape _____

   Formula _____

   Solution _____

2. Mrs. Sorenson wants to put a green border around her bulletin board. The bulletin board is 6 ft by 4 ft. How many feet of border will she need?

   Shape _____

   Formula _____

   Solution _____

   Go on to the next page.

Perimeter and Area Formulas, page 2

Helpful formulas:

Perimeter

P = sum of lengths of sides (any polygon)

$P = 2l + 2w$ (rectangle)

$P = 4s$ (square)

Area

$A = lw$ (rectangle)

$A = s^2$ (square)

$A = \frac{1}{2} bh$ (triangle)

Directions Solve each problem. Explain the steps you took. ✏

3. For his project, Louis needs a triangular piece of wood that has a base of 25 cm and a height of 16 cm. How many square centimeters of wood is that?

   Shape _____

   Formula _____

   Solution _____

4. Nellie is putting a new floor in her kitchen. If her kitchen is 18 ft by 22 ft, how many square feet of flooring will she need?

   Shape _____

   Formula _____

   Solution _____

5. Stephanie is planting flowers on the border of her triangular garden. The garden is 6 feet on each side. How many feet of flowers will she need to plant?

   Shape _____

   Formula _____

   Solution _____

6. Chris is building a frame for a painting. The painting is 24 inches on each side. How many inches of framing material will he need?

   Shape _____

   Formula _____

   Solution _____

7. Colin is painting a small triangular piece of wood that is 5 inches long and 6 inches high. What is the area of this piece of wood?

   Shape _____

   Formula _____

   Solution _____

Circles

To find the circumference of a circle, use the formula $C = \pi d$. In the formula, d is the diameter of the circle. Use 3.14 for π. To find the area of a circle, use the formula $A = \pi r^2$. In the formula, r is the radius of the circle. The radius of the circle is equal to half the diameter.

Here's How!

Step 1: Read the problem.
Jerry has a picture in the shape of a circle. The diameter is 8 cm. What is the circumference?

Step 2: Choose the correct formula.
$C = \pi d$

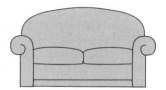

Step 3: Replace π with 3.14 and d with 8 and solve.
$C = 3.14 \times 8$
$C = 25.12$
The circumference of the picture is 25.12 inches.

Directions Solve each problem. Explain the steps you took.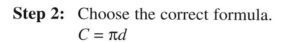

1. A furniture store delivers without charge to any location within a 100-mile radius of the store. What is the area of this region?

   _____

   _____

2. A circular wagon wheel has a diameter of 14 inches. What is the circumference of the wheel?

   _____

   _____

3. A cherry pie has a radius of 5 inches. What is the area of the pie?

   _____

   _____

Go on to the next page.

Circles, page 2

To find the circumference of a circle, use the formula $C = \pi d$. In the formula, d is the diameter of the circle. Use 3.14 for π. To find the area of a circle, use the formula $A = \pi r^2$. In the formula, r is the radius of the circle. The radius of the circle is equal to half the diameter.

Directions Solve each problem. Explain the steps you took.

4. A cellular phone tower receives signals from a 60-mile radius. What is the area covered by the tower's receiver?

_____

_____

5. A circular pie pan has a radius of 6 inches. What is the circumference?

_____

_____

6. A tabletop has a diameter of 60 inches. What is the circumference of this round tabletop?

_____

_____

7. A small pizza has a diameter of 8 inches. What is the area of the small pizza?

_____

_____

8. A cow is tied on a 50-foot rope. The cow can graze on any of the grass it can reach. What is the area on which the cow can graze?

_____

_____

9. A farm has a circular pond with a 40-foot radius. What is the area of the pond?

_____

_____

10. Martha grew a pumpkin with a diameter of 18 inches. What is the circumference of the pumpkin?

_____

_____

Surface Area of Boxes

A box is a 3-dimensional figure that has width, depth, and height. On a rectangular box, there are 6 surface areas. The top and bottom are the same size, the front and back are the same size, and the sides are the same size. To find the total surface area of the box, you must find the area of the top, front, and side. Add these areas, then multiply by 2 to find the total surface area.

Here's How!

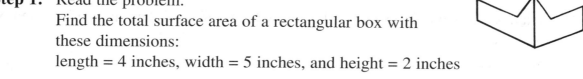

Step 1: Read the problem.
Find the total surface area of a rectangular box with these dimensions:
length = 4 inches, width = 5 inches, and height = 2 inches

Step 2: Find the areas of the top, front, and side.
Area of the top = 5 × 4 = 20 square inches
Area of the front = 5 × 2 = 10 square inches
Area of the side = 4 × 2 = 8 square inches

Step 3: Add the areas together.
20 + 10 + 8 = 38 square inches

Step 4: Multiply the total by 2.
38 × 2 = 76 square inches
The rectangular box has a total surface area of 76 square inches.

Directions ➡ Solve each problem. Explain the steps you took. ✐

1. A rectangular box is 6 inches wide, 12 inches long, and 8 inches high. What is the total surface area of the box?

   _____

   _____

2. A square box, called a cube, has a height of 5 inches. What is the total surface area of the cube?

   _____

   _____

   Go on to the next page.

Surface Area of Boxes, page 2

Directions Solve each problem. Explain the steps you took. ✏️

3. Mrs. Tate is wrapping presents for her grandchildren in a rectangular box that is 24 in. by 10 in. by 16 in. What is the total surface area of the box?

_____

_____

4. Jessica has a box that is 18 cm by 12 cm by 6 cm. What is the total surface area of Jessica's box?

_____

_____

5. Mike received a box in the mail that was 3 ft by 4 ft by 2 ft. What is the total surface area of Mike's box?

_____

_____

6. Jan is looking for a box that measures 7 in. by 20 in. by 10 in. What is the total surface area of the box Jan needs?

_____

_____

7. Jason is wrapping a friend's birthday present. The box is 20 in. by 16 in. by 12 in. What is the total surface area of the box?

_____

_____

8. Nancy has a box that 4 cm on each side. What is the total surface area of the box?

_____

_____

Name _____ Date _____

Volumes of Boxes

Volume is the amount of space inside a 3-dimensional object. Volume is measured in cubic units. To find the volume of a rectangular box, use the formula $V = l \times w \times h$.

Here's How!

Step 1: Read the problem.
What is the volume of a rectangular box with a length of 4 inches, a width of 5 inches, and a height of 6 inches?

Step 2: Replace l with 4, w with 5, and h with 6.
$V = l \times w \times h$
$V = 4 \times 5 \times 6$
$V = 120$ cubic inches
The volume of the box is 120 cubic inches.

Directions Solve each problem. Explain the steps you took. ✎

1. A rectangular box has a height of 6 inches, a width of 10 inches, and a length of 7 inches. What is the volume of the box?

_____

_____

2. A square box, a cube, has a width of 4 inches. What is the volume of the cube?

_____

_____

3. A small shed has a width of 10 feet, a length of 12 feet, and a height of 8 feet. What is the volume of the shed?

_____

_____

Go on to the next page.

Name _____   Date _____

Volumes of Boxes, page 2

Directions Solve each problem. Explain the steps you took. ✏

4. A cube has a height of 7 inches. What is the volume of the cube?

_____

_____

5. For a party, Helen cut a block of cheese into 3-in by 3-in by 1-in pieces. What is the volume of each piece?

_____

_____

6. Tim wants to store his younger brother's building blocks, which are 1 inch by 4 inches by 6 inches. What is the volume of each block?

_____

_____

7. Mark is building a box that is 5 feet by 2 feet by 4 feet. What is the volume of the box?

_____

_____

8. The Martins are digging a hole for their swimming pool that is 40 feet by 20 feet by 12 feet. What is the volume of the hole?

_____

_____

9. A cereal company sells cereal in a box that is 5 inches by 12 inches by 2 inches. What is the volume of the box?

_____

_____

10. Jeff is filling a box that is 7 inches by 5 inches by 3 inches. What is the volume of the box?

_____

_____

Name _____ Date _____

Volumes of Cylinders

To find the volume of a cylinder, use the formula $V = \pi r^2 h$. You multiply the area of the base, a circle, by the height. Use 3.14 for π. You may use a calculator.

Here's How!

Step 1: Read the problem.
What is the volume of a cylinder with a radius of 4 inches and a height of 6 inches?

Step 2: Replace π with 3.14, r with 4, and h with 6.
$V = \pi r^2 h$
$V = 3.14 \times 4^2 \times 6$
$V = 3.14 \times 16 \times 6$
$V = 50.24 \times 6$
$V = 301.44$
The volume of the cylinder is 301.44 cubic inches.

Directions **Solve each problem. Explain the steps you took.** ✐

1. Find the volume of a cylinder with a radius of 2 inches and a height of 4 inches.

_____

_____

_____

2. Find the volume of a cylinder with a radius of 5 inches and a height of 3 inches.

_____

_____

3. Find the volume of a cylinder with a radius of 7 inches and a height of 2 inches.

_____

_____

_____

4. Find the volume of a cylinder with a radius of 8 inches and a height of 3 inches.

_____

_____

_____

Go on to the next page.

Volumes of Cylinders, page 2

To find the volume of a cylinder, use the formula $V = \pi r^2 h$. You multiply the area of the base, a circle, by the height. Use 3.14 for π. You may use a calculator.

Directions **Solve each problem. Explain the steps you took.** ✏️

5. Sylvia is making a flower arrangement. She wants to fill a cylindrical vase with water. The vase is 18 inches tall and has a radius of 3 inches. How much water will the vase hold?

_____

_____

_____

6. Robert made a cylinder to hold his marbles. The cylinder is 14 inches high and has a radius of 3 inches. What is the volume of the cylinder?

_____

_____

_____

7. Frank is filling a cylindrical jar with jelly. The cylinder is 6 inches high and has a radius of 2 inches. What is the volume of the cylinder?

_____

_____

_____

8. Eddie is filling a coffee can with coffee beans. If the can is 10 inches high and has a radius of 4 inches, what is the volume of the can?

_____

_____

_____

Name _____ Date _____

Unit 4 Assessment: Measurement

Directions → Solve each problem. Explain the steps you took. ✏️

1.   6 hr 24 min
    + 3 hr 57 min

_____

_____

_____

2. Allison has 0.76 m of ribbon. Debbie has 248 cm of ribbon. Who has more? How much more?

_____

_____

_____

3. Joe poured 48 mL of paint into a 3-L paint can. How many more mL of paint does he need to fill the can?

_____

_____

_____

4. Ethan has 2 pieces of rope. One piece is 4 ft 7 in. long and the other is 5 ft 10 in. long. How much rope does Ethan have altogether?

_____

_____

_____

5. Gretchen drank 14 quarts of juice in February. She drank 3 gallons in March. During which month did she drink more?

_____

_____

_____

Name _____ Date _____

Money Relationships

Converting between types of currency is an important skill. In the United States, the currency is the U.S. dollar. Italian currency is called the *lire*, British currency is called the *pound*, Swiss currency is called the *franc*, and German currency is called the *mark*. To find out how much the U.S. dollar is worth in another country's currency, you must find the exchange rate.

1 U.S. dollar =
3.5 German marks
2,000 Italian lire
0.5 British pound
2.5 Swiss francs

Here's How!

Step 1: Read the problem.
You want to buy postcards in Germany. If each postcard costs 1 mark, and you have $3.00 to spend, how many postcards can you buy?

Step 2: Find the exchange rate.
1 U.S. dollar = 3.5 German marks

Step 3: Solve the problem.
3.5 marks per dollar × 3 dollars = 10.50 marks
You can buy 10 postcards.

Directions Solve each problem. Explain the steps you took. ✏

1. In Switzerland, your father buys a watch for 375 francs. What is its price in U.S. currency?

_____

2. When you leave Switzerland, you have 10 francs left. You want to exchange the Swiss francs for Italian lire. How many lire will you receive?

_____

3. You buy a statuette of the Leaning Tower of Pisa in Italy and a stuffed bear in England. The statuette costs 9,000 lire and the bear costs 5 pounds. How much does each item cost in U.S. dollars?

_____

4. In England you see a cassette tape that sells for 3.5 pounds. You have seen the same cassette in the United States for $5.50. Is it less expensive in the United States or in England?

Time

You can use the fact that 60 min = 1 hr to help you rename when adding and subtracting intervals of time.

Here's How!

Example 1:

Step 1: Find the sum.

    8 hr 25 min
  + 3 hr 47 min
   11 hr 72 min

Step 2: Rename.

72 min = 1 hr 12 min
11 hr 72 min =
11 hr + 1 hr 12 min =
12 hr 12 min

Example 2:

Step 1: Find the difference.

   13 hr 16 min
  − 4 hr 25 min
Since 16 < 25, rename 13 hr 16 min

Step 2: Rename.

13 hr 16 min =
12 hr 60 min + 16 min =
12 hr 76 min

Step 3: Solve.

   12 hr 76 min
  − 4 hr 25 min
    8 hr 51 min

Directions Solve each problem. Explain your steps as you go. ✎

1.   7 hr 30 min
  + 6 hr 35 min

2.   10 hr 42 min
  + 5 hr 28 min

3.   17 hr 22 min
  − 9 hr 35 min

4.   7 hr 27 min
  − 4 hr 38 min

5.   2 hr 20 min
  − 1 hr 35 min

6.   11 hr 17 min
  + 11 hr 44 min

7. Debbie spent 1 hr 20 min in the pool on Monday and 2 hr 5 min on Tuesday. What total length of time was she in the pool?

_____

8. Each morning it takes Pete 1 hr 15 min to meet with his employees and 30 min to answer messages. How much longer does Pete spend in meetings than answering messages?

_____

Metric Length

You can use the facts that 1 km = 1,000 m and 1 m = 100 cm to convert between kilometers, meters, and centimeters.

Here's How!

Step 1: Read the problem.
Rich has 536 m of rope. Sam has 5.25 km of rope.
Who has the longer piece of rope? By how much?

Step 2: Convert 5.25 km to m.
$5.25 \times 1,000 = 5,250$
Sam has 5,250 m of rope.

Step 3: Compare the lengths.
5,250 m > 536 m
Sam has the longer piece of rope.

Step 4: Subtract to find how much longer.
$5,250 - 536 = 4,714$
Sam's piece is 4,714 m longer.

Directions Solve each problem. Explain the steps you took. ✏️

1. Barbara has 0.27 km of ribbon. Sue has 325 m of ribbon. Who has more ribbon? How much more?

   _____

   _____

2. Tina bought 5 m of string for a project. She used 135 cm of the string. How much string does she have left?

   _____

   _____

   _____

Go on to the next page.

Metric Length, page 2

You can use the facts that 1 km = 1,000 m and 1 m = 100 cm to convert between kilometers, meters, and centimeters.

Directions Solve each problem. Explain the steps you took. ✏

3. Mary ran 6.35 km. Janet ran 3,250 m. Who ran farther? How much farther?

_____

_____

_____

4. John is 2.56 m tall. Trevor is 178 cm tall. Who is taller? How much taller?

_____

_____

5. Cody can throw a ball 325 m. Trent can throw a ball 0.300 km. Who can throw farther? How much farther?

_____

_____

_____

6. Jason drove 325 km. Mark drove 4,281 m. Who drove farther? How much farther?

_____

_____

_____

Metric Capacity

You can use the fact that 1 L = 1,000 mL to convert between liters and milliliters.

Here's How!

Step 1: Read the problem.
The capacity of a small glass is 100 mL. How many small glasses can be filled from a 1-L pitcher?

Step 2: Convert 1 L to milliliters.
1 L = 1,000 mL

Step 3: Divide the capacity of the pitcher by the capacity of the glass.
1,000 ÷ 100 = 10
10 small glasses can be filled from a 1-L pitcher.

Directions Solve each problem. Explain your steps as you go.

1. If Mrs. Jensen fills her watering can with 1,750 mL of water, how many liters is she using?

   _____

   _____

   _____

2. Philip poured 0.25 L of juice into each of 4 glasses. How many mL of juice is in each glass?

   _____

   _____

   _____

3. Rachel poured 55 mL of juice into a 2-L pitcher. How many mL of juice must she add to fill the pitcher?

   _____

   _____

   _____

Go on to the next page.

Metric Capacity, page 2

You can use the fact that 1 L = 1,000 mL to convert between liters and milliliters.

Directions ▸ Solve each problem. Explain the steps you took. ✏

4. A restaurant uses 2,000 milliliters of cherry juice each day. How long does it take the restaurant to use up a 14-L bottle?

_____

_____

_____

5. The volume of a juice carton is 960 mL. How many liters of juice does it hold?

_____

_____

_____

6. A jug of grape juice is 3.5 L. What is the capacity of the jug in milliliters?

_____

_____

_____

7. Kevin is making lemonade from a powdered mix. The container says one scoop of powder will make 750 mL. How many scoops are needed to make 3 L?

_____

_____

_____

8. The capacity of a small bowl is 250 milliliters. How many small bowls can be filled from a 2-L container?

_____

_____

_____

Name _____ Date _____

Customary Length

You can use the fact that 12 inches = 1 foot to help you rename when adding and subtracting customary units of length.

Here's How!

Example 1:
Step 1: Find the sum.

    4 ft   3 in.
 + 5 ft 10 in.
    9 ft 13 in.

Step 2: Rename.
13 in. = 1 ft 1 in.
9 ft 13 in. = 9 ft + 1 ft 1 in. =
10 ft 1 in.

Example 2:
Step 1: Find the difference.

    5 ft 4 in.
 − 2 ft 7 in.
Since 4 < 7, rename 5 ft 4 in.

Step 2: Rename.
5 ft 4 in. = 4 ft 12 in. + 4 in. =
4 ft 16 in.

Step 3: Solve.

    4 ft 16 in.
 − 2 ft 7 in.
    2 ft 9 in.

Directions → Solve each problem. Explain your steps as you go. ✏️

1.   11 ft 4 in.
    + 2 ft 9 in.

2.   9 ft 4 in.
    − 4 ft 6 in.

3.   7 ft 3 in.
    − 4 ft 4 in.

4.   4 ft 4 in.
    + 1 ft 8 in.

5.   4 ft
    − 1 ft 2 in.

6.   4 ft 5 in.
    + 3 ft 7 in.

Go on to the next page.

Customary Length, page 2

You can use the fact that 12 inches = 1 foot to help you rename when adding and subtracting customary units of length.

Directions Solve each problem. Explain your steps as you go.

7. Christy has two pieces of ribbon. One piece is 3 ft 4 in. and the other is 2 ft 9 in. How much ribbon does she have altogether?

_____

_____

_____

8. Evan has a piece of rope that is 6 ft 4 in. He needs to cut off a piece that is 3 ft 10 in. How much rope will he have left?

_____

_____

_____

9. Riley is 2 ft 4 in. tall. He must be 4 ft 2 in. tall to ride the rides at the amusement park. How much taller must he grow?

_____

_____

_____

10. Shane was 5 ft 5 in. at the beginning of the school year. He grew to 6 ft 1 in. by the end of the school year. How much did he grow?

_____

_____

_____

Customary Capacity

The chart below will help you convert between customary units of capacity.

| 8 fluid ounces (fl oz) = 1 cup (c) |
| 2 c = 1 pint (pt) |
| 2 pt = 1 quart (qt) |
| 4 qt = 1 gallon (gal) |

Here's How!

Step 1: Read the problem.
Cora used 3 gallons of milk one week. The next week she used 16 quarts. During which week did she use more?

Step 2: Convert 3 gallons to quarts.
1 gal = 4 qt
3 gal = 12 qt

Step 3: Compare the two capacities.
16 qt > 12 qt
She used more milk the second week.

Directions Solve each problem. Explain the steps you took.

1. 148 qt = _____ gal

2. 33 pt = _____ qt _____ pt

3. 12 qt 3 pt = _____ pt

4. 13 gal = _____ qt

5. 12 c = _____ fl oz

6. 320 fl oz = _____ c

7. 5 qt 3 pt = _____ pt

8. 28 pt = _____ qt

9. 20 c = _____ pt

10. 12 pt = _____ c

Go on to the next page.

Name _____ Date _____

Customary Capacity, page 2

The chart below will help you convert between customary units of capacity.

> 8 fluid ounces (fl oz) = 1 cup (c)
> 2 c = 1 pint (pt)
> 2 pt = 1 quart (qt)
> 4 qt = 1 gallon (gal)

Directions Solve each problem. Explain the steps you took.

11. Mandy and her mother were doing the laundry. Each load uses 10 fl oz of liquid detergent. If they have 1 qt of detergent, how many loads can they do?

_____

_____

_____

12. Julie is dyeing T-shirts purple. She needs 6 c of dye for each T-shirt. If she wants to dye 3 T-shirts, how many pints of dye does she need?

_____

_____

_____

13. Carol has a 1-qt carton of orange juice. Does she have enough juice to fill four 8-oz glasses?

_____

_____

_____

14. Tammy uses 32 cups of pudding in her recipe for making pies. How many quarts of pudding does she use?

_____

_____

_____

Unit 5 Assessment: Data Analysis and Probability

Directions Solve each problem. Explain the steps you took.

1. Garrett has 5 marbles. Two are red, 2 are green, and 1 is blue. If Garrett chooses a marble at random, what is the probability Garrett will choose a red marble?

   _____

   _____

   _____

2. David had 4 shirts, 3 pairs of pants, and 2 belts. How many combinations of 1 shirt, 1 pair of pants, and 1 belt can he make?

   _____

   _____

   _____

3. Make a Venn Diagram to show the following data.
   Of the 30 students surveyed, 10 play only basketball, 12 play only baseball, and 5 play both basketball and baseball. Three students do not play either sport.

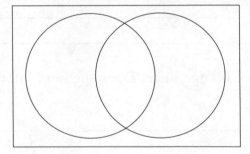

4. Use the circle graph to answer the question.
   If $\frac{1}{5}$ of the pencils in the store are mechanical pencils, what percent of the store's inventory is made up of mechanical pencils?

   _____

   _____

   _____

   _____

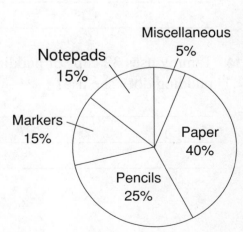

Name _____ Date _____

Probability

Probability is used to predict the chances of different events happening. Probability can be written as a fraction.

Here's How!

Step 1: Read the question.

Suppose you have 2 blue marbles and 3 pink marbles in a bag. If you don't look in the bag, what is the probability you will choose a pink marble?

Step 2: Write a fraction.

$$\frac{3 \text{ pink marbles}}{5 \text{ total marbles}}$$

The probability of choosing a pink marble is $\frac{3}{5}$.

Directions Solve each problem. Explain the steps you took.

1. Each person at Judy's party rolls a number cube. The numbers on the cube are 1 to 6. What is the probability Judy will roll a 3?

   _____

   _____

   _____

2. Jeffrey has 5 blue balloons and 1 red balloon in a sack. If he chooses a balloon without looking, what is the probability a blue balloon will be chosen?

   _____

   _____

   _____

3. Ben, Nancy, Hank, and Shane are playing a board game. To see who goes first, they write their names on pieces of paper and put them into a box. What is the probability that Shane will get to go first?

   _____

   _____

   _____

Go on to the next page.

Probability, page 2

Directions Solve each problem. Explain the steps you took. ✏

4. Ben needs to roll a 6 on a number cube to win the game. What is the probability of rolling a 6?

   _____

   _____

5. Nancy must roll a 1 or 2 or she will lose. What are Nancy's chances of rolling 1 or 2 in one roll?

   _____

   _____

6. Hank is about to land on Lose-a-Turn. He must roll a 1, 2, or 6 on the number cube to avoid this space. What is the probability he will roll one of these numbers?

   _____

   _____

7. Shane lands on a free space. He must roll a 1, 2, or 3 to earn extra points. What is the probability he will roll these numbers?

   _____

   _____

8. Ben lost all of his tokens, so he is out of the game. What is the probability Hank will win?

   _____

   _____

Combinations

Combinations are made by finding all the different ways to group a set of items. To find how many combinations can be made, multiply the number of first choices by the number of second choices.

Here's How!

Step 1: Read the problem.
Mark has 4 sweaters and 3 shirts that can be worn in any combination. How many shirt-sweater combinations can he make?

Step 2: Multiply the number of sweaters by the number of shirts.
$4 \times 3 = 12$
Mark can make 12 shirt-sweater combinations.

To show how this works, you can use a tree diagram.

```
                  Shirt A ——— 1
Sweater A  ———  Shirt B ——— 2
                  Shirt C ——— 3

                  Shirt A ——— 4
Sweater B  ———  Shirt B ——— 5
                  Shirt C ——— 6

                  Shirt A ——— 7
Sweater C  ———  Shirt B ——— 8
                  Shirt C ——— 9

                  Shirt A ——— 10
Sweater D  ———  Shirt B ——— 11
                  Shirt C ——— 12
```

Which method is easier to use?

Directions Solve each problem. Explain the steps you took.

1. David had 5 kinds of crackers and 4 kinds of cheese. How many cracker-cheese combinations can he make?

_____

Go on to the next page.

Combinations, page 2

Directions Solve each problem. Explain the steps you took. ✏

2. The cafeteria at Easton Middle School
   is serving a choice of 4 entrees,
   4 vegetables, and 2 desserts. How
   many combinations of 1 entree,
   1 vegetable, and 1 dessert can
   be made?

   _____

3. Students at Northside Intermediate
   School are holding student-council
   elections. Three people are running for
   president, 3 people are running for
   vice-president, and 4 are running for
   treasurer. How many possible
   combinations of student-council
   officers are there?

   _____

4. Chris has 5 long-sleeved shirts and
   3 pairs of pants to mix and match.
   How many combinations can he make?

   _____

5. A restaurant offers 5 different kinds of
   pasta and 6 different sauces. How
   many combinations of pasta and sauce
   can the restaurant make?

   _____

6. Matthew has 4 shirts, 5 ties, and 3 hats.
   How many combinations of 1 shirt,
   1 tie, and 1 hat can he make?

   _____

Making Venn Diagrams

A Venn diagram shows the relationships among different sets of things.

Here's How!

Step 1: Read the problem.
The Weekly Farm Report found that of 200 farms, 80 have only cows, 60 have only sheep, 40 have both, and 20 have neither.

Step 2: Fill in the diagram to show the data.

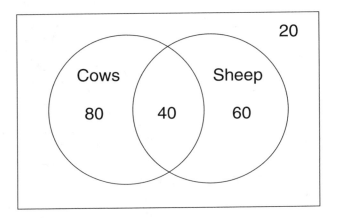

Directions **Make a Venn diagram to show the given data. Explain the steps you took.** ✏️

1. An animal shelter shows that of the 100 families that come in looking for a pet, half adopt a cat and a dog. Six adopt no animals and the number of families that adopt only a cat is the same as those who adopt only a dog.

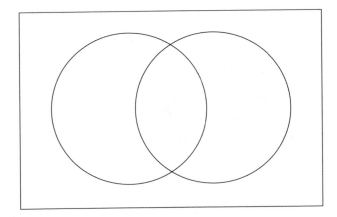

Go on to the next page.

Making Venn Diagrams, page 2

Directions ➡ Make a Venn diagram to show the given data. Explain the steps you took. ✎

2. Of 350 ranches, 150 have only horses, 100 have only cows, 75 have no animals, and 25 have both horses and cows.

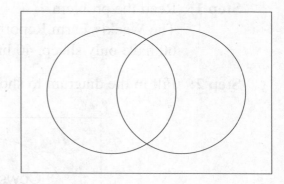

3. Of the 50 students surveyed at school, 25 own only dogs, 10 own only cats, and 5 own both. Eight students own only fish, and 2 students own all three.

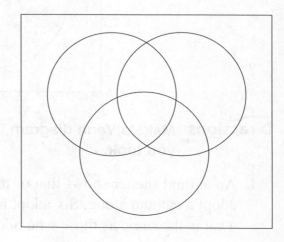

4. At the Lots of Pets pet store, 45 people bought fish last week. Ten bought only red fish, 15 bought only yellow fish, and 9 bought only blue fish. Two people bought a red and a blue fish, 5 people bought a red and a yellow fish, and 1 person bought a blue and a yellow fish. Three people bought all 3 colors of fish.

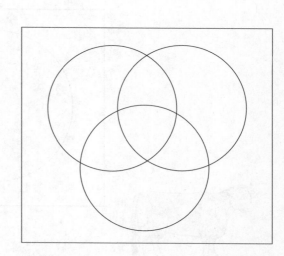

Misleading Line Graphs

Line graphs can often be misleading. A break in the scale of the graph can make a graph appear differently without changing the data.

Here's How!

Step 1: Examine the graphs.

Step 2: Read the problem.

Graph A shows the number of flights Express Airlines chartered over a 9-month period. Express Airlines wants to emphasize how fast the company has grown in 9 months. Does the graph make this point?

Graph B presents the same data. Does the graph emphasize the rapid increase in flights chartered on Express Airlines as effectively as the previous graph?

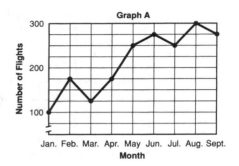

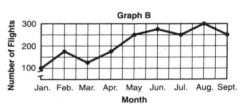

Directions ▶ Solve each problem. Explain the steps you took. ✎

1. How many CDs were sold during Week 1 in January? in July?

   _____

2. How many CDs were sold during Week 3 in January? in July?

   _____

3. What is the difference in the number of CDs sold during Week 1 and Week 3 in January?

   _____

4. What is the difference in the number of CDs sold during Week 1 and Week 3 in July?

   _____

5. Which graph makes the difference between Week 1 and Week 3 appear greater? Explain.

   _____

Go on to the next page.

Misleading Line Graphs, page 2

Directions Solve each problem. Explain the steps you took. ✏️

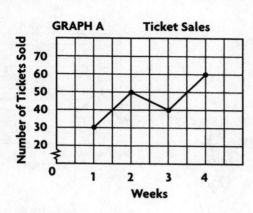

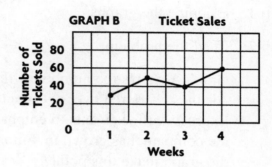

6. In Graph A, how many times as great as the sales in Week 1 do the sales in Week 4 appear?

_____

7. In Graph B, about how many times as great as the sales in Week 1 do the sales in Week 4 appear?

_____

8. What was the actual difference in sales between Week 1 and Week 4 for each graph?

_____

9. Were Week 4 sales 2.5 times as great?

_____

10. Which graph gives a better picture of the data?

_____

11. Are the data in a misleading graph factual?

_____

12. Explain what makes a graph appear misleading.

_____

Name _____ Date _____

Circle Graphs

A circle graph compares parts of a whole. Percents are often used to represent these parts. The percents will add up to 100.

Here's How!

Step 1: Read the problem.
Lined paper makes up 60% of the paper inventory. What percentage of the store's inventory is made up of lined paper?

Step 2: Examine the circle graph.
Notice that paper is 40%.

Step 3: Write a number sentence and solve. Remember to change the percent to a decimal.
60% of 40% is what?
0.60 x 0.40 = 0.24
24% of the store's inventory is made up of lined paper.

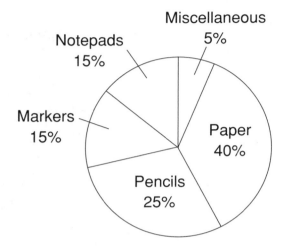

Directions ➡ Solve each problem. Explain the steps you took.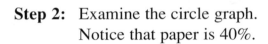

1. Which item makes up the most of the store's inventory?

   _____

2. What percentage of the inventory is made up of items other than paper?

   _____

3. The store's inventory is worth $460.00. How much are the markers worth?

   _____

4. The store's inventory is worth $460.00. How much are notepads and pencils worth together?

   _____

5. What percentage of the inventory is made up of markers?

   _____

Go on to the next page.

Circle Graphs, page 2

Directions Solve each problem. Explain the steps you took. ✏️

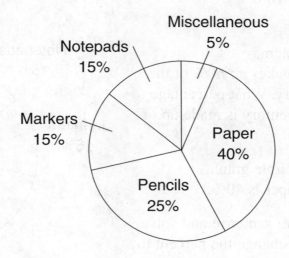

Miscellaneous 5%
Notepads 15%
Markers 15%
Paper 40%
Pencils 25%

6. The store stocks twice as many large notepads as small notepads. What percentage of the inventory is made up of large notepads?

   _____

7. Does the store stock more paper or more pencils and markers together?

   _____

8. Do paper and pencils make up more than or less than half of the inventory?

   _____

9. If miscellaneous items do not include any paper products, what percentage of the inventory includes nonpaper items?

   _____

10. The School Store makes a 30% profit on everything it sells. The entire inventory cost $345 to stock. How much profit would be made if the entire inventory was sold?

    _____

Multistep Math with Written Explanations, Grade 6
Answer Key

Note: Answer explanations will vary. Accept all reasonable explanations. Possible answers are given.

pp. 3–4

1. $3 + 8 - 4 - 2 = n$; $5 = n$; Haley left the elevator on the 5th floor. Start on the 3rd floor. Add 8 for up 8 floors, subtract 4 for down 4 floors, and subtract 2 for down 2 floors.
2. 92; Add the scores for his first 4 tests. Multiply the average of all 5 tests by 5. $425 - 333 = 92$
3. 4, 3(4), 12; 6, 3(6), 18; 8, 3(8), 24; Replace w with the values and simplify.
4. $60.00; $80.00 × 25\% = $20.00; $80.00 - $20.00 = $60.00
5. 310 sq in.; $5 × 7 = 35$, $7 × 10 = 70$, and $5 × 10 = 50$. $35 + 70 + 50 = 155$; $155 × 2 = 310$
6. 24,727.5 cu in.; $V = \pi r^2 h$, $V = 3.14(15)^2(35)$
7. 1 hr 28 min; Rename 3 hr 16 min as 2 hr 76 min. Subtract the hours and minutes.
8. the green string; 25m; $0.075 \text{ km} × 1,000 = 75 \text{ m}$ $75 > 50$, $75 - 50 = 25$
9. $\frac{3}{7}$; There are 3 green hats so 3 is the numerator. There are 7 total hats so 7 is the denominator.
10. 30 combinations; $2 × 3 × 5 = 30$

p. 5

1. $4 + 5 - 2 - 1 = n$; $6 = n$; Betsy left the elevator on the sixth floor. Start on the fourth floor. Add 5 for up 5 floors, subtract 2 for down 2 floors and subtract 1 for down 1 floor.
2. 11; Multiply 2 by 3 first, then add 5 to the result.
3. 76; Add the scores on his first 4 games. Multiply the average of all 5 games by 5. $80 × 5 = 400$. Subtract $400 - 324 = 76$.
4. 525 miles; 225 miles ÷ 3 hours = 75 miles per hour. 75 miles per hour × 7 hours = 525 miles
5. 5; $3\frac{3}{4} ÷ \frac{3}{4} = 5$.

pp. 6–7

1. $1 + 6 - 2 = n$; $5 = n$; Josh ended up on the 5th floor. Start on the 1st floor. Add 6 for up 6 floors, and subtract 2 for down 2 floors.
2. $12 - 2 + 4 = n$; $14 = n$; Rich left the elevator on the 14th floor. Start on the 12th floor. Subtract 2 for down 2 floors, and add 4 for up 4 floors.
3. $3 + 8 - 2 + 3 = n$; $12 = n$; Jim exited on the 12th floor. Start on the 3rd floor. Add 8 for up 8 floors, subtract 2 for down 2 floors, and add 3 for up 3 floors.
4. $9 + 5 - 6 - 2 = n$; $6 = n$; James left on the 6th floor. Start on the 9th floor. Add 5 for up 5 floors, subtract 6 for down 6 floors, and subtract 2 for down 2 floors.
5. $1 + 14 - 6 + 4 = n$; $13 = n$; Christina exited on the 13th floor. Start on the 1st floor. Add 14 for up 14 floors, subtract 6 for down 6 floors, and add 4 for up 4 floors.
6. $5 - 1 - 3 + 4 = n$; $5 = n$; Evan left on the 5th floor. Start on the 5th floor. Subtract 1 for down 1 floor, subtract 3 for down 3 floors, and add 4 for up 4 floors.
7. $1 + 6 - 3 + 2 = n$; $6 = n$; Carly exited on the 6th floor. Start on the 1st floor. Add 6 for up 6 floors, subtract 3 for down 3 floors, and add 2 for up 2 floors.
8. $5 + 3 - 2 = n$; $6 = n$; Erica left the elevator on the 6th floor. Start on the 5th floor. Add 3 for up 3 floors, and subtract 2 for down 2 floors.

pp. 8–9

1. 5; Add 4 and 6 first, then divide the result by 2. $4 + 6 = 10$; $10 ÷ 2 = 5$
2. 23; Multiply 3 by 5 first, then add 8. $3 × 5 = 15$; $15 + 8 = 23$
3. 2; Add 3 and 8 first, then subtract 9. $3 + 8 = 11$; $11 - 9 = 2$

4. 20; Subtract 6 from 10 first, then multiply by 5. $10 - 6 = 4$; $4 × 5 = 20$
5. 0; Multiply 3 by 2 first, then subtract the result from 6. $3 × 2 = 6$; $6 - 6 = 0$
6. 2; Add 1 and 1 first, then divide 4 by the result. $1 + 1 = 2$; $4 ÷ 2 = 2$
7. 6; Subtract 6 from 8 first, then add 4. $8 - 6 = 2$; $2 + 4 = 6$
8. 13; Multiply 2 and 3 first, then subtract the result from 19. $2 × 3 = 6$; $19 - 6 = 13$
9. 3; Add 4 and 1 first, then divide 15 by the result. $4 + 1 = 5$; $15 ÷ 5 = 3$
10. 5; Add 8 and 2 first, then divide by 2. $8 + 2 = 10$; $10 ÷ 2 = 5$
11. 36; Subtract 9 from 18, then multiply by 4. $18 - 9 = 9$; $9 × 4 = 36$
12. 24; Divide 6 by 2 first, then multiply by 8. $6 ÷ 2 = 3$; $3 × 8 = 24$
13. $(8 + 3) × 5$; Add 8 and 3 first, then multiply by 5 to get 55. $8 + 3 = 11$; $11 × 5 = 55$

pp. 10–11

1. 87; Add the scores on her first 4 tests. Multiply the average by 5. Subtract the first result from the second.; $425 - 338 = 87$
2. 146; Add the scores on his first 4 games. Multiply the average by 5. Subtract the first result from the second.; $600 - 454 = 146$
3. 76; Add the scores on his first 5 rounds. Multiply the average by 6. Subtract the first result from the second.; $450 - 374 = 76$
4. 100; Add the scores on his first 5 tests. Multiply the average by 6. Subtract the first result from the second.; $540 - 440 = 100$
5. 126; Add the scores on her first 5 games. Multiply the average by 6. Subtract the first result from the second.; $720 - 594 = 126$
6. 284; Add the numbers for the first 6 showings. Multiply the average by 7. Subtract the first result from the second.; $1,960 - 1,676 = 284$
7. 72; Add the numbers for the first 5 buses. Multiply the average by 6. Subtract the first result from the second.; $420 - 348 = 72$
8. 90; Add the grades for the first 5 six weeks. Multiply the average by 6. Subtract the first result from the second.; $540 - 450 = 90$

pp. 12–13

1. 216 mi; 4 trips × 9 miles per trip = 36 miles; 36 miles × 6 days = 216 miles
2. 396 mi; 132 miles × 2 = 264 miles; 264 miles + 132 miles = 396 miles
3. 216 pictures; 12 rolls – 3 rolls = 9 rolls; 9 rolls × 24 pictures per roll = 216 pictures
4. 6 days; 4 miles per hour × 7 hours = 28 miles; 168 miles ÷ 28 miles = 6 days
5. 9 drivers; 450 miles each day × 5 days = 2,250 miles; 2,250 miles ÷ 250 miles = 9 drivers
6. 14 hours; 186 miles ÷ 3 hours = 62 miles per hour; 868 miles ÷ 62 miles per hour = 14 hours
7. 45 miles; 18 miles × 5 days = 90 miles to find Jack's total distance. 18 ÷ 2 = 9 to find Sam's distance per day. 9 miles × 5 days = 45 miles to find Sam's total distance; 90 miles – 45 miles = 45 miles
8. 3,675 miles; 1,575 miles ÷ 3 hours = 525 miles per hour; 525 mile per hour × 7 hours = 3,675 miles

pp. 14–15

1. 5 servings; $3\frac{1}{3} ÷ \frac{2}{3} = 5$
2. $\frac{1}{24}$ hr; $3\frac{1}{2}$ hours $+ 2\frac{3}{4}$ hours $= 6\frac{1}{12}$ hours to find Dave's hours. $1\frac{5}{8}$ hours $+ 4\frac{1}{2}$ hours $= 6\frac{1}{8}$ hours to find Colleen's hours. $6\frac{1}{8}$ hours $- 6\frac{1}{12}$ hours $= \frac{1}{24}$ hour
3. 7 servings; $9\frac{1}{3} ÷ 1\frac{1}{3} = 7$
4. $1\frac{5}{8}$ ft; $1\frac{1}{2} + 2\frac{1}{4} = 3\frac{3}{4}$; $5\frac{3}{8} - 3\frac{3}{4} = 1\frac{5}{8}$
5. $\frac{7}{15}$ hr; $1\frac{1}{2} + \frac{1}{5} = 1\frac{7}{10}$; $2\frac{1}{6} - 1\frac{7}{10} = \frac{7}{15}$
6. $\frac{1}{2}$; $\frac{2}{7} + \frac{3}{14} = \frac{1}{2}$; $1 - \frac{1}{2} = \frac{1}{2}$
7. 6 loads; $7\frac{1}{2} ÷ 1\frac{1}{4} = 6$
8. $\frac{1}{9}$; $\frac{1}{3} + \frac{5}{9} = \frac{8}{9}$; $1 - \frac{8}{9} = \frac{1}{9}$

p. 16

1. 12, 12 − 5, 7; 14, 14 − 5, 9; 16, 16 − 5, 11
2. $n + 5 = 7$; $n = 2$
3. $0.33; $0.31; The 12-pack of juice boxes; Divide the price by the number of boxes.
4. $18; $\frac{4}{24} = \frac{3}{x}$; $x = 8$
5. $60.00; $75.00 × 20% = $15.00. $75.00 − $15.00 = $60.00.
6. $29.43; $27.50 × 7% = $1.93; $1.93 + $27.50 = $29.43

pp. 17–18

1. 7, 7 + 3, 10; 8, 8 + 3, 11; 9, 9 + 3, 12
2. 13, 13 − 8, 5; 15, 15 − 8, 7; 19, 19 − 8, 11
3. 7, 4(7), 28; 8, 4(8), 32; 9, 4(9), 36
4. 18, 18 ÷ 6, 3; 24, 24 ÷ 6, 4; 36, 36 ÷ 6, 6
5. 8, 8 + 25, 33; 12, 12 + 25, 37; 16, 16 + 25, 41
6. 8, 8 − 7, 1; 12, 12 − 7, 5; 16, 16 − 7, 9
7. 8, 3(8), 24; 12, 3(12), 36; 16, 3(16), 48
8. 8, 8 ÷ 4, 2; 12, 12 ÷ 4, 3; 16, 16 ÷ 4, 4
9. 8, 2(8) + 1, 17; 12, 2(12) + 1, 25; 16, 2(16) + 1, 33
10. 8, 3(8) − 2, 22; 12, 3(12) − 2, 34; 16, 3(16) − 2, 46

pp. 19–20

1. $r − 3 = 8$; $r = 11$
2. $5k = 25$; $k = 5$
3. $5 + u = 14$; $u = 9$
4. $\frac{w}{3} = 7$; $w = 21$
5. $\frac{d}{6} = 48$; $d = 288$
6. $w − 33 = 40$; $w = 73$
7. $\frac{f}{7} = 12$; $f = 84$
8. $14 + c = 18.3$; $c = 4.3$
9. $2k = 36$; $k = 18$
10. $r + 6.3 = 12.5$; $r = 6.2$
11. $2h = 56$; $h = 28$
12. $m + 7 = 18$; $m = 11$

pp. 21–22

1. Addition; $37 + 45 = n$, $n = 82$ pictures
2. Multiplication; $48 × 2 = n$, $n = 96$ minutes
3. Multiplication; $36 × 2 = n$, $n = 72$ sandwiches
4. Division; $40 ÷ 8 = n$; $n = 5$ people
5. Division; $60 ÷ 5 = n$; $n = 12$ people
6. Multiplication; $28 × 5 = n$; $n = 140$ people
7. Subtraction; $25 − 8 = n$; $n = 17$ fossils
8. Multiplication; $4 × 3 = n$; $n = 12$ people

pp. 23

1. $0.31 per bar; Divide the price by the number of bars. $1.24 ÷ 4 = $0.31
2. $0.33 per pen; Divide the price by the number of pens. $0.99 ÷ 3 = $0.33
3. $0.58 per bottle; Divide the price by the number of bottles. $6.96 ÷ 12 = $0.58
4. $0.16 per bar; Divide the price by the number of bars. $1.28 ÷ 8 = $0.16
5. $0.99 per pound, $0.85 per pound; the 10-pound box; Divide the price by the number of pounds. $4.95 ÷ 5 = $0.99, $8.50 ÷ 10 = $0.85
6. $0.12, $0.11; the package of 8; Divide the price by the number of buns. $1.44 ÷ 12 = $0.12, $0.88 ÷ 8 = $0.11
7. $0.93, $0.89; the package of 6; Divide the price by the number of lightbulbs. $3.72 ÷ 4 = $0.93, $5.34 ÷ 6 = $0.89
8. $0.09, $0.10; the 6-ounce can; Divide the price by the number of ounces. $0.54 ÷ 6 = $0.09, $1.60 ÷ 16 = $0.10

9. $0.08, $0.09; the box of 10 envelopes; Divide the price by the number of ounces. $0.80 ÷ 10 = $0.08, $1.08 ÷ 12 = $0.09
10. $0.82, $0.79; the set of 10 glasses; Divide the price by the number of glasses. $6.56 ÷ 8 = $0.82, $7.90 ÷ 10 = $0.79
11. $0.03, $0.04; the 36-ounce bottle; Divide the price by the number of ounces. $1.08 ÷ 36 = $0.03, $0.48 ÷ 12 = $0.04

p. 24

1. $60.25; $22.00 × 2 = $44.00 for the cost of 2 wool skirts. $44.00 + $8.75 + $7.50 = $60.25
2. $3.00; $10.00 × 2 = $20.00 for the cost of 10 pairs of socks. $7.50 × 2 = $15.00 for the cost of 2 scarves. $20.00 + $15.00 + $12.00 = $47.00; $50.00 − $47.00 = $3.00
3. $42.50; $11.00 × 3 = $33.00 for the cost of 3 ties. $33.00 + $9.50 = $42.50
4. $17.01; $17.00 × 3 = $51.00 for the cost of 3 pairs of corduroy pants. $51.00 − $33.99 = $17.01
5. $25.75; $14.00 × 3 = $42.00 for the cost of 3 umbrellas. $42.00 + $8.75 = $50.75; $50.75 − $25.00 = $25.75

p. 25

1. $4; $\frac{5}{1} = \frac{20}{x}$, $x = 4$
2. $2\frac{1}{2}$ quarts; $\frac{1}{4} = \frac{x}{10}$, $x = 2\frac{1}{2}$
3. 45 min; $\frac{2}{30} = \frac{3}{x}$, $x = 45$
4. $504, $\frac{56}{4} = \frac{x}{36}$, $x = 504$
5. 350 sq ft; $\frac{618}{100} = \frac{2,163}{x}$, $x = 350$
6. $140; $\frac{2}{25} = \frac{x}{1,750}$, $x = 140

p. 26

1. $8.17; $24.52; $32.69 × 25% = $8.17; $32.69 − $8.17 = $24.52
2. $21.45; $85.80; $107.25 × 20% = $21.45; $107.25 − $21.45 = $85.80.
3. $7.43; $42.07; $49.50 × 15% = $7.43; $49.50 − $7.43 = $42.07
4. $29.75; $119.00; $148.75 × 20% = $29.75; $148.75 − $29.75 = $119.00

p. 27

1. $1.06; $22.31; $21.25 × 5% = $1.06; $21.25 + $1.06 = $22.31
2. $2.63; $46.38; $43.75 × 6% = $2.63; $43.75 + $2.63 = $46.38
3. $1.54; $40.04; $38.50 × 4% = $1.54; $38.50 + $1.54 = $40.04
4. $5.54; $74.79; $69.25 × 8% = $5.54; $69.25 + $5.54 = $74.79

p. 28

1. 168 in.; Use the perimeter of a rectangle formula. $P = 2l + 2w$; $P = 2(36) + 2(48) = 168$
2. 113.04 sq ft; Use the area of a circle formula. $A = \pi r^2$; $A = 3.14(6)^2 = 113.04$
3. 304 sq in; Find the areas of the top, front, and side. $8 × 4 = 32$, $4 × 10 = 40$, $8 × 10 = 80$; Add them together. $32 + 40 + 80 = 152$; Multiply the result by 2. $152 × 2 = 304$
4. 125 cu in; Use the volume of a cube formula $V = l × w × h$; $V = 5 × 5 × 5 = 125$
5. 502.4 cu in.; Use the volume of a cylinder formula $V = \pi r^2 h$; $V = 3.14(4)^2(10) = 502.4$

pp. 29–30

1. square; $A = s^2$; 25 sq ft
2. rectangle; $P = 2l + 2w$; 20 ft
3. triangle; $A = \frac{1}{2}bh$; 200 sq cm
4. rectangle; $A = lw$; 396 sq ft
5. triangle; P = sum of lengths of sides; 18 ft
6. square; $P = 4s$; 96 in.
7. triangle; $A = \frac{1}{2}bh$; 15 sq in.

pp. 31–32

1. 31,400 sq mi; $A = \pi r^2$; $A = 3.14(100)^2 = 31,400$
2. 43.96 in.; $C = \pi d$; $C = 3.14(14) = 43.96$
3. 78.5 sq in.; $A = \pi r^2$; $A = 3.14(5)^2 = 78.5$
4. 11,304 sq mi; $A = \pi r^2$; $A = 3.14(60)^2 = 11,304$
5. 37.68 in.; $C = \pi d$; $C = 3.14(12) = 37.68$
6. 188.4 in.; $C = \pi d$; $C = 3.14(60) = 188.4$
7. 50.24 sq in.; $A = \pi r^2$; $A = 3.14(4)^2 = 50.24$
8. 7,850 sq ft; $A = \pi r^2$; $A = 3.14(50)^2 = 7,850$
9. 5,024 sq ft; $A = \pi r^2$; $A = 3.14(40)^2 = 5,024$
10. 56.52 in.; $C = \pi d$; $C = 3.14(18) = 56.52$

pp. 33–34

1. 432 sq in.; Multiply to find the areas of the front, side, and top. $6 \times 12 = 72$, $12 \times 8 = 96$, $6 \times 8 = 48$; Add the results together. $72 + 96 + 48 = 216$; Multiply the new result by 2. $216 \times 2 = 432$
2. 150 sq in.; Multiply 5×5 three times. $5 \times 5 = 25$; Add the results. $25 + 25 + 25 = 75$; Multiply the new result by 2. $75 \times 2 = 150$
3. 1,568 sq in.; Multiply to find the areas of the front, side, and top. $24 \times 10 = 240$, $10 \times 16 = 160$, $24 \times 16 = 384$; Add the results. $240 + 160 + 384 = 784$; Multiply the new result by 2. $784 \times 2 = 1,568$
4. 792 sq cm; Multiply to find the areas of the front, side, and top. $18 \times 12 = 216$, $12 \times 6 = 72$, $18 \times 6 = 108$; Add the results. $216 + 72 + 108 = 396$; Multiply by 2. $396 \times 2 = 792$
5. 52 sq ft; Multiply to find the areas of the front, side, and top. $3 \times 4 = 12$, $4 \times 2 = 8$, $3 \times 2 = 6$; Add the results. $12 + 8 + 6 = 26$; Multiply the new result by 2. $26 \times 2 = 52$
6. 820 sq in.; Multiply to find the areas of the front, side, and top. $7 \times 20 = 140$, $20 \times 10 = 200$, $7 \times 10 = 70$; Add the results. $140 + 200 + 70 = 410$; Multiply the new result by 2. $410 \times 2 = 820$
7. 1,504 sq in.; Multiply to find the areas of the front, side, and top. $20 \times 16 = 320$, $16 \times 12 = 192$, $20 \times 12 = 240$; Add the results. $320 + 192 + 240 = 752$; Multiply the new result by 2. $752 \times 2 = 1,504$
8. 96 sq cm; Multiply 4×4 three times. $4 \times 4 = 16$; Add the results. $16 + 16 + 16 = 48$; Multiply the new result by 2. $48 \times 2 = 96$

pp. 35–36

1. 420 cu in.; $6 \times 10 \times 7 = 420$
2. 64 cu in.; $4 \times 4 \times 4 = 64$
3. 960 cu ft; $10 \times 12 \times 8 = 960$
4. 343 cu in.; $7 \times 7 \times 7 = 343$
5. 9 cu in.; $3 \times 3 \times 1 = 9$
6. 24 cu in.; $1 \times 4 \times 6 = 24$
7. 40 cu ft; $5 \times 2 \times 4 = 40$
8. 9,600 cu ft; $40 \times 20 \times 12 = 9,600$
9. 120 cu in.; $5 \times 12 \times 2 = 120$
10. 105 cu in.; $7 \times 5 \times 3 = 105$

pp. 37–38

1. 50.24 cu in.; $V = \pi r^2$, $V = 3.14(2)^2(4)$
2. 235.5 cu in.; $V = \pi r^2$, $V = 3.14(5)^2(3)$
3. 307.72 cu in.; $V = \pi r^2$, $V = 3.14(7)^2(2)$
4. 602.88 cu in.; $V = \pi r^2$, $V = 3.14(8)^2(3)$
5. 508.68 cu in.; $V = \pi r^2$, $V = 3.14(3)^2(18)$
6. 395.64 cu in.; $V = \pi r^2$, $V = 3.14(3)^2(14)$
7. 75.36 cu in.; $V = \pi r^2$, $V = 3.14(2)^2(6)$
8. 502.4 cu in.; $V = \pi r^2$, $V = 3.14(4)^2(10)$

p. 39

1. 10 hr 21 min; Add the hours and minutes. Rename 9 hr 81 min to 10 hr 21 min.
2. Debbie; 172cm; $0.76 \times 100 = 76$ to change from m to cm. $248 > 76$; $248 - 76 = 172$
3. 2,952 mL; $3 \times 1,000 = 3,000$ to convert L to mL. $3,000 - 48 = 2,952$

4. 10 ft 5 in.; Add the feet and inches. Rename 9 ft 17 in. to 10 ft 5 in.
5. February; $3 \times 4 = 12$ to convert gallons to quarts. $14 > 12$

p. 40

1. $150; $375 \div 2.5 = 150
2. 8,000 lire; $10 \div 2.5 = 4$; $4 \times 2,000 = 8,000$
3. $4.50, $10.00; $9,000 \div 2,000 = 4.5$ to find the cost of the statuette. $5 \div 0.5 = 10$ to find the cost of the bear.
4. It is less expensive in the United States.; $3.5 \div 0.5 = 7$ to find the price in dollars. Compare the amounts.

p. 41

1. 14 hr 5 min; Add the hours and minutes. Rename 65 min to 1 hr 5 min.
2. 16 hr 10 min; Add the hours and minutes. Rename 70 min to 1 hr 10 min.
3. 7 hr 47 min; Rename 17 hr 22 min to 16 hr 82 min. Subtract the hours and minutes.
4. 2 hr 49 min; Rename 7 hr 27 min to 6 hr 87 min. Subtract the hours and minutes.
5. 45 min; Rename 2 hr 20 min to 1 hr 80 min. Subtract the hours and minutes.
6. 23 hr 1 min; Add the hours and minutes. Rename 22 hr 61 min to 23 hr 1 min.
7. 3 hr 25 min; Add the hours and minutes.
8. 45 min; Rename 1 hr 15 min to 75 min. Subtract the minutes.

pp. 42–43

1. Sue; 0.055 km; $325 \div 1,000 = 0.325$ to convert m to km.
2. 365 m; $5 \times 100 = 500$ to convert m to cm; $500 - 135$
3. Mary; 3,100 km; $6.35 \times 1,000 = 6,350$ to convert km to m. $6,350 > 3,250$; $6,350 - 3,250 = 3,100$
4. John; 78 cm; $2.56 \times 100 = 256$ to convert m to cm. $256 > 178$; $256 - 178 = 78$
5. Cody; 25 m; $0.300 \times 1,000 = 300$ to convert km to m. $325 > 300$; $325 - 300 = 25$
6. Jason; 320.719 km; $4,281 \div 1,000 = 4.281$ to convert m to km. $325 > 4.281$; $325 - 4.281 = 320.719$

pp. 44–45

1. 1.75 L; $1,750 \div 1,000 = 1.75$
2. 250 mL; $0.25 \times 1,000 = 250$
3. 1,945 mL; $2 \times 1,000 = 2,000$ to convert L to mL. $2,000 - 55 = 1,945$
4. 7 days; $2,000 \div 1,000 = 2$ to convert mL to L. $14 \div 2 = 7$
5. 0.96 L; $960 \div 1,000$ to convert to L.
6. 3,500 mL; $3.5 \times 1,000 = 3,500$ to convert to mL.
7. 4 scoops; $3 \times 1,000 = 3,000$ to convert to mL. $3,000 \div 750 = 4$
8. 8 bowls; $250 \div 1,000 = 0.250$ to convert to L. $2 \div 0.25 = 8$

pp. 46–47

1. 14 ft 1 in.; Add the feet and inches. Rename 13 ft 13 in. to 14 ft 1 in.
2. 4 ft 10 in.; Rename 9 ft 4 in. to 8 ft 16 in. Subtract the feet and inches.
3. 2 ft 11 in.; Rename 7 ft 3 in. to 6 ft 15 in. Subtract the feet and inches.
4. 6 ft; Add the feet and inches. Rename 5 ft 12 in. to 6 ft.
5. 2 ft 10 in.; Rename 4 ft to 3 ft 12 in. Subtract the feet and inches.
6. 8 ft; Add the feet and inches. Rename 7 ft 12 in. to 8 ft.
7. 6 ft 1 in.; Add the feet and inches. Rename 5 ft 13 in. to 6 ft 1 in.
8. 2 ft 6 in.; Rename 6 ft 4 in. to 5 ft 16 in. Subtract the feet and inches.
9. 1 ft 10 in.; Rename 4 ft 2 in. to 3 ft 14 in. Subtract the feet and inches.
10. 8 in.; Rename 6 ft 1 in. to 5 ft 13 in. Subtract the feet and inches.

pp. 48–49
1. 37 gal; 148 quarts ÷ 4 quarts per gallon = 37 gal
2. 16 qt 1 pt; 33 pt ÷ 2 pt per qt = 16 qt R 1; The remainder is 1 pt.
3. 27 pt; 12 qt × 2 pt per qt = 24 pt; Add 3 pt to the result.
4. 52 qt; 13 gal × 4 qt per gal = 52 qt
5. 96 fl oz; 12 c × 8 oz per cup = 96 oz
6. 40 c; 320 fl oz ÷ 8 oz per cup = 40 c
7. 13 pt; 5 qt × 2 pt per qt = 10 pt; Add 3 pt to the result.
8. 14 qt; 28 pt ÷ 2 pt per qt = 14 qt
9. 10 pt; 20 c ÷ 2 c per pt = 10 pt
10. 24 c; 12 pt × 2 cups per pt = 24 c
11. 3 loads; Convert 1 qt to ounces. 1 qt = 2 pt = 4 c = 32 oz; 32 oz ÷ 10 oz = 3 R 2.
12. 9 pt; 6 c per shirt × 3 shirts = 18 cups; 18 cups ÷ 2 cups per pt = 9 pt
13. Yes; Convert 1 qt to ounces; 1 qt = 2 pt = 4 c = 32 oz; 4 glasses × 8 ounces = 32 oz. Compare the results.
14. 8 qt; 32 cups ÷ 2 cups per pt = 16 pt; 16 ÷ 2 = 8

Pg 50
1. $\frac{2}{5}$; Two of the marbles are red so 2 is the numerator. There are 5 total marbles so 5 is the denominator.
2. 24; 4 × 3 × 2 = 24
3.

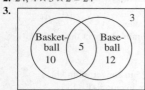

4. 5%; $\frac{1}{5}$ = 0.2; 0.25 × 0.2 = 0.05

pp. 51–52
1. $\frac{1}{6}$; There is only one 3 on a number cube so 1 is the numerator. There are 6 sides to a cube, so 6 is the denominator.
2. $\frac{5}{6}$; There are 5 blue balloons, so 5 is the numerator. There are 6 total balloons, so 6 is the denominator.
3. $\frac{1}{4}$; There is one Shane, so 1 is the numerator. There are 4 total names, so 4 is the denominator.
4. $\frac{1}{6}$; There is one 6 on the number cube, so 1 is the numerator. There are 6 sides on the number cube, so 6 is the denominator.
5. $\frac{1}{3}$; There are 2 numbers to choose from, so 2 is the numerator. There are 6 sides on the number cube, so 6 is the denominator. $\frac{2}{6} = \frac{1}{3}$
6. $\frac{1}{2}$; There are 3 numbers to choose from, so 3 is the numerator. There are 6 sides on the number cube, so 6 is the denominator. $\frac{3}{6} = \frac{1}{2}$
7. $\frac{1}{2}$; There are 3 numbers to choose from, so 3 is the numerator. There are 6 sides on the number cube, so 6 is the denominator. $\frac{3}{6} = \frac{1}{2}$
8. $\frac{1}{3}$; There is only one Hank, so 1 is the numerator. Since Ben is out, there are only 3 players, so the denominator is 3.

pp. 53–54
1. 20; 5 × 4 = 20
2. 32; 4 × 4 × 2 = 32
3. 36; 3 × 3 × 4 = 36
4. 15; 5 × 3 = 15
5. 30; 5 × 6 = 30
6. 60; 4 × 5 × 3 = 60

pp. 55–56
1.

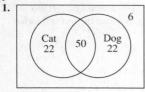

2.

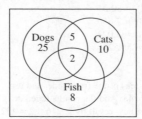

3.

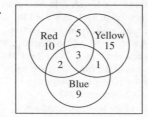

4.

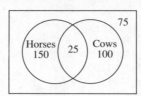

pp. 57–58
1. 30; 60
2. 66, 100
3. 36
4. 40
5. January; The intervals in the January graph are 12, while the intervals in the July graph are 20.
6. 2.5 times as great
7. twice as great
8. 30
9. No, they were twice as great.
10. Graph B; the intervals are the same on the scale.
11. Yes, the data are factual. The presentation is misleading.
12. Size of scale; whether or not there is a break in the axis.

pp. 59–60
1. Paper; 40% is the largest percent.
2. 60%; 5% + 15% + 15% + 25% = 60%
3. $69.00
4. $184.00
5. 15%
6. 10%; 15% ÷ 3 = 5%. Two of the parts are large notebooks and one is small notebooks.
7. The same amount of paper as pencils and markers.
8. More than half. 40% + 25% = 65%; 65% is more than half.
9. 45%; 5% + 15% + 25% = 45%
10. $103.50; $345 × 30% = $103.50.